HOW TO TRAIN YOUR HUSBAND

An Owner's Manual

TAMMY L BROWN

1

This book is dedicated to my mother who tried so hard to train me. Sorry Mom, it just didn't "take".

Introduction

The faint sound of running water wakes me in the middle of the night. I stumble half-asleep to the bathroom, nearly falling into the toilet bowl as the seat is up...again. Welcome to the wonderful world of husband training, where we attempt to civilize the uncivilized man-child into a semi-respectable life partner.

This manual will provide all the tools and techniques you'll need to train your husband in the basics of cohabitation. From aiming his pee into the toilet bowl instead of onto the floor, to putting his dirty socks in the hamper rather than leaving them for you to pick up, we've got you covered. Consider this the dog training guide...but for the grown man who still behaves like an unruly puppy.

Sit. Stay. Don't pee on the rug. The commands may seem harsh, but they could save your marriage when your husband insists on acting like an untrained animal. Patience and persistence are key. Reward good behavior with treats and affection. Scold poor behavior by squirting him with a spray bottle or blowing an obnoxious whistle. And remember, you can't expect him to learn overnight. Much like housebreaking a new puppy, husband training takes time.

But once he masters the basics like lifting the toilet seat up AND down, you'll be ready to move onto more advanced techniques, like loading the dishwasher properly or folding laundry without mangling everything. This isn't about nagging or nitpicking. It's about working together to create a happy home. Consider this manual a lighthearted guide to strengthening your bond through communication and teamwork. Now grab your spray bottle and whistle…it's time to get training!

Let's start by diving into the topics this manual will cover to bring more laughter and levity into your relationship."

Inside you'll find tips, tricks, and tongue-in-cheek advice on:

- Toilet Seat Etiquette 101: Getting him to put the seat down every time

- Dishwasher Loading for Novices: Achieving the perfect optimized pack

- Laundry Folding: Smoothing those wrinkled edges once and for all

- Dress Code Debacles: Convincing him your advice is on point

- Movie Night Negotiations: Compromising on genres you both enjoy

- Driving Directions: When to help navigate and when to just let him drive

- Clothing Combinations: Mixing and matching his wardrobe into stylish looks

- Sports Stats: Nodding along to his team trivia and analysis

- BBQ Mastery: Coaching the perfect steak or burger

- Household Chore Mediation: Getting to a fair division of labor

- And much more!

The chapters ahead promise equal parts education and entertainment. You'll learn proven techniques to improve your husband's habits while enjoying some laughs along the journey. With a healthy dose of patience and a whole lot of love and humor, you'll be on your way to strengthening your bond and having fun together.

So, turn the page and let's dive into Husband Training 101

I know what you're thinking - husband training sounds silly or even impossible. But I'm here to tell you it can be done! With some creativity, mutual understanding, and yes, a good sense of humor, you can guide your husband towards positive change.

I mean, no one's perfect, right? But we can all strive to be a little bit better for our partners. And if we approach it from a place of love and support rather than criticism, our chances improve exponentially.

At the end of the day, it's not about molding your man into an ideal husband. It's about communicating openly, compromising when needed, and working together to build the relationship you both deserve. One filled with laughter, comfort, and growing trust.

So don't be afraid to embark on this journey with me. With patience and positivity, we'll get your husband trained in no time! And we'll have a whole lot of fun along the way. Turn the page, and let's get started!

Chapter 1

The Wild Creature

I awake with a jolt, my bladder screaming. Bleary-eyed, I stumble down the dark hallway. The bathroom door is closed, but a sliver of light peeks out from underneath. Of course, he's in there.

I rap my knuckles against the door. "Honey, you in there?"

"Yep!" comes the muffled reply.

"Any chance you're wrapping up?"

"Sorry babe, gonna be a minute!"

"Take your time hon, I only birthed 4 of your little bastards, my bladder is just fine and dandy!"

I squeeze my thighs together and dance in place. A minute is an eternity when your bladder is about to explode.

The toilet flushes, the sink runs, and finally the door opens. As my husband steps out, a wave of relief washes over me. I bolt past him into the bathroom.

Then, as I careen across the floor, slipping and sliding in a puddle of piss, damn near breaking my neck, while soaking my socks, I see it. The toilet seat, mockingly upright.

This man, this creature I married. So quick to lift the seat for his own convenience, but never lowers it for mine.

I sigh, then perform the awkward toilet seat shuffle - half squat, lean, lower, hover. Why must I go through this ritual every time? Can he not take two seconds to lower the seat when he's done? Must I decode the inner workings of the male brain, just to take care of a basic bodily function?

As I wash my hands, I stare into the mirror. Someday, I will train this man. But for now, I'll embrace our differences. Opposites attract, right?

I shut off the faucet and head back to bed, making a mental note to stop for caffeine on my way to the office tomorrow. I'll need it after this late-night bathroom battle. Maybe I'll pick up a toilet seat extender too. Baby steps.

I emerge from the bathroom, shaking my head at yet another toilet seat debacle. As I crawl back into bed, my husband stirs.

"Everything okay, honey?" he mumbles sleepily.

"Oh yes, just peachy," I reply. "Thanks for leaving the seat up again."

He blinks in confusion. "What's the big deal? You can put it back down."

I sigh. "It's the principle. Why should I have to move it every time?"

"I don't know, I just...pee and go. Not a lot of thought happens at 2am," he says with a shrug.

Clearly, we need to have a little talk about peeing in public. Or rather, not peeing in public. I know he means well, but some things require more forethought.

"Sweetie, remember last weekend at the fair when you had to pee so badly you ran behind the hot dog stand? Or when we were hiking and you watered that poor sapling?" I ask.

His eyes widen. "You said you wouldn't bring that up again!"

"Well, I'm bringing it up. You must stop the public urination. It's a crime!"

He frowns. "But when you gotta go..."

"You hold it!" I interject. "Do you know they make portable urinals for men? Or just use a bottle in the car if you must. But please, no more peeing outside."

"Fine, fine," he concedes. "I'll work on it."

*WARNING - that is code for the male species - TRANSLATION - "If you will shut up at this exact moment, I will be more strategic in hiding this disgusting habit from you until a later date when I think you might have rethought your position and then and only then will I 'whip it out' in public once again."

"Thank you," I reply. "It's for the greater good. I'm just trying to civilize you."

He laughs and pulls me closer. "Good luck with that."

Though we're different, I know we'll figure this out. I'll decode this man yet. Even if it takes all night.

"Now, speaking of territorial instincts," I say, segueing to the next topic, "I couldn't help but notice you've been a bit possessive with the remote control lately."

He frowns. "What? No, I haven't."

"Oh really?" I counter. "So, you didn't hide it under your pillow last night when I wanted to watch my show?"

"I have no idea what you're talking about," he says, avoiding eye contact.

"Uh huh. And I suppose the remote just happened to be on your side of the bed every single time we watched TV this week?" I press.

He shifts uncomfortably. "Fine, you got me. I like having the remote close by. Is that such a crime?"

I soften my tone. "Of course not, sweetie. I get it, the remote is your way of marking your territory. It's a guy thing."

He looks relieved that I understand.

"But maybe we can compromise?" I suggest gently. "Like, you can keep the remote on your side of the bed when we watch your shows, and I'll keep it on my side when it's my turn to pick what we watch."

He considers this. "I guess that could work."

"Great!" I say. "It's all about give and take in a relationship."

He smiles and pulls me in for a kiss. Though we still have much to learn about each other, with understanding and compromise, we'll make this work.

"Now, I know giving up total control of the remote is a big sacrifice for you," I say playfully. "So how about we make you a nice 'man cave' in the basement where you can retreat with your remote and gadgets when you need some alone time?"

He lights up at this suggestion. "A man cave? For real?"

I laugh at his excitement. "Yes, for real! We can get you a big comfy recliner, mount a huge TV on the wall, and deck out the space with all your favorite toys."

"That sounds amazing!" he says dreamily.

"And in return, you'll relinquish dominion over the living room remote when I ask nicely, right?" I add with a wink.

"Deal!" he agrees enthusiastically, pulling me in for another kiss.

Though compromise doesn't always come easy, a little creativity and understanding goes a long way. By giving my husband space to indulge his territorial instincts, and getting some remote-free time to myself, we've struck a balance that meets both our needs. As different as men and women may be, with some effort, we can bridge the divide.

I take a deep breath as I move on to the next topic. Who cares if it is 3am? I feel like I'm finally making some headway and for once he seems receptive. Discussing the language barrier between men and women is tricky territory, but if we're going to make this relationship work, it's time to confront the elephant in the room.

"Communication is the foundation of any healthy relationship," I start, treading lightly so as not to put him on the defensive. "But sometimes, no matter how hard we try, there are still misunderstandings between us."

My husband instantly tenses. He knows where this is going.

"Like the other day," I continue. "When I asked if you could stop at the store on the way home, and you came back with beer and chips. Meanwhile I was waiting for ingredients to make dinner."

I force an awkward laugh, hoping humor will diffuse the tension. He scratches his head, searching for the right words. I feel bad putting him on the spot, but we have to work through this.

"I guess I didn't connect the dots," he mumbles. "I thought you just wanted me to pick up some snacks."

"Right, that's exactly the issue," I say gently. "We interpreted that request completely differently."

I touch his arm reassuringly. As frustrating as these situations are, getting upset won't help. We stare at each other in silence, contemplating this stark example of our frequent miscommunications. If we're going to make this work, we both have some learning to do about understanding each other's language.

I take a deep breath and launch into my advice. "So here are a few things we can try to avoid confusion going forward. First, anytime I ask you to get something at the store, I'll be very specific about what I need. Grocery list in writing, no more vague requests."

He nods, seeming relieved at the straightforward suggestion.

"And it wouldn't hurt for both of us to use more visual aids," I continue. "Like sending example photos of what we're talking about by text."

"That's not a bad idea," he agrees.

"We could even take it up a notch and resort to interpretive dance!" I exclaim, twirling around the bedroom dramatically. I shimmy and gesticulate, miming household tasks. He cracks up watching my ridiculous performance.

"Alright, alright, I get your point," he chuckles, as I dive on him mid-pirouette.

As we embrace, giggling uncontrollably, I feel optimistic. With some creativity and commitment to understand each other better, we can bridge this language divide. The differences between men and women may sometimes feel vast, but love conquers all barriers.

Chapter 2

The Training Toolbox

Laughter is the Best Medicine

The most essential tool in any husband training toolkit is a sense of humor. Without the ability to laugh at the inevitable mishaps, mix-ups and mistakes that will occur throughout the training process, frustration can easily set in on both sides. But when approached with a spirit of lightheartedness and fun, husband training becomes an enjoyable bonding experience for both trainer and trainee.

As your husband slowly begins to master the basic commands - "sit", "stay", "roll over" - accidents are bound to happen. Maybe he enthusiastically rolls off the bed during an overzealous "roll over" command. Or perhaps he springs up from "stay" too soon and trips over his own feet. While these blunders could seem annoying, they present the perfect opportunity for some much-needed comic relief.

So, when your husband inevitably goofs up a command, surprise him by bursting into laughter instead of scolding him. Watch how the embarrassed look on his face melts into relief and delight at your reaction. This shared moment of levity strengthens your connection and makes the process more fun for you both. Laughter relieves tension, puts mistakes into perspective, and paves the way for future success. With a chuckle and a smile, even the most clueless husband's antics can be endearing rather than exasperating.

Approached with gentle humor and patience, husband training will blossom into a rewarding path of growth and intimacy. A hearty dose of laughter makes the journey more amusing, and the bond more unshakeable. So, grab your toolkit, strap on your sense of humor, and get ready to laugh your way to marital bliss!

Here is more of the scene:

"Oh no, not again!" I sighed as I walked into the kitchen. There was my husband, covered head to toe in flour. The countertop looked like a snowstorm had blown through.

"I was just trying to make you cookies," he said sheepishly.

I couldn't help but chuckle. This wasn't the first kitchen mishap he'd had recently. Just last week he got caught peeing in the kitchen sink. And who could forget the time he somehow managed to get spaghetti stuck to the ceiling?

"It's the thought that counts," I said, giving him a kiss on the cheek and leaving a faint flour handprint behind.

He grinned, knowing I wasn't actually upset. I'd come to realize these disasters were just part of what made him so endearingly hapless. And meeting them with patience and humor made it easier to take in stride.

"How about I help you clean up and we order takeout instead?" I suggested.

He nodded eagerly. "That sounds perfect."

As we wiped the flour off the counters, I laughed again thinking about the sight that had greeted me. Moments like these were exasperating but also hilarious, bringing us closer through shared amusement. And I must admit, his determination to try baking for me despite his lack of skill was admirable.

With laughter, patience and a few paper towels, we tidied up the kitchen and his adorably botched attempt at domesticity. And I knew there would be many more silly misadventures to come in our future together.

I nodded, taking a deep breath to gather my patience. As much as I wanted to scold him for the mess, I knew that wouldn't be productive.

"You're right, yelling won't help. Let's clean this up together." I said evenly, handing him a rag.

He looked relieved, dabbing at a blob of batter on the floor.

I reminded myself that change takes time. My husband wasn't going to transform into a master chef overnight. But with consistent, positive reinforcement, he could get there eventually.

Rather than criticizing his crumbling cookies, I decided to focus on the intention behind it. He had wanted to do something thoughtful. And that deserved acknowledgement, even if the execution was a disaster.

"I really appreciate you trying to make me something special." I said. "How about next time, we cook together? I can show you some tricks."

His eyes lit up and he nodded eagerly. "Yeah, that sounds great! I want to learn how to make all your favorites."

I smiled, my heart warmed. With patience and teamwork, we would get there. No training method works overnight. But the reward of gradual progress through mutual understanding makes it all worthwhile.

As we cleaned, I thought about other tips for cultivating patience in our relationship.

"Sometimes when I'm feeling frustrated, it helps if I take a few deep breaths to calm down," I suggested. "Or if I go into another room for a minute to collect myself."

"That's a great idea," my husband replied. "And maybe I could try that mindfulness app you use. The one with the nature sounds and stuff."

"Absolutely!" I said. "Practicing mindfulness is so helpful for dealing with stressful situations."

I made a mental note to send him the link to download the app later. Baby steps like that can gradually strengthen patience over time.

When the kitchen was finally spotless again, I pulled my husband in for a hug. "Even when things get messy, we'll get through it together," I said. "As long as we lead with love and understanding."

He hugged me back tightly. "You really are the most patient and caring wife ever. I'm so lucky to be with you."

I smiled up at him, feeling hopeful. With continued compassion and teamwork, we would be unstoppable.

After we finished cleaning the kitchen, I decided it was a perfect opportunity to introduce the concept of positive reinforcement.

"Although I still have no clue how it happened, I know I was pretty frustrated earlier today when you spilled the Diet Coke in the oven," I began. "But I want you to know I really appreciate you sticking with it and helping me clean everything up. I know it wasn't fun, but working together as a team means so much to me."

My husband's face lit up at the praise. "Aww, thanks babe! I'm glad I could help."

I went on, "And since you were such a trooper, how about I cook your favorite meal tonight - my special chicken tetrazzini?"

"Oh wow, you're the best!" he exclaimed. "I can't wait."

I smiled, pleased that the positive reinforcement was already working its magic. I decided to keep going and drove the point home.

"You see, positive reinforcement is so much more effective than criticism or punishment when it comes to relationship training. It's all about focusing on the good behavior you want to see more of and rewarding it."

My husband nodded along enthusiastically. "That makes total sense. It's way better than being yelled at or something."

"Exactly," I agreed. "It creates a positive atmosphere that encourages lasting change."

I gave him another big hug, proud of the progress we were making. With continued positivity and mutual understanding, we were well on our way to relationship bliss.

"Now, I know some old-school relationship guides recommend using shock collars or other negative reinforcement techniques," I continued. "But studies have shown those approaches often backfire by creating fear, anxiety, or resentment in the trainee."

My husband's eyes widened. "Wow, shock collars? That sounds horrible!"

"I know, right?" I said. "Imagine being zapped every time you make a little mistake. You'd be walking on eggshells, too afraid of messing up to act naturally."

He shuddered. "Yeah, that would suck. I'd probably get pissed off and want to rebel."

"Exactly," I said. "Whereas with positive reinforcement, you feel supported and encouraged to keep improving."

I could see the lightbulb going off in his head as he absorbed this insight.

"When you put it that way, positive reinforcement is definitely the way to go," my husband agreed. "I want us to be happy together, not for me to be scared of you."

I smiled and squeezed his hand warmly. "That's music to my ears. Now, who's ready to help me start prepping for that chicken tetrazzini?"

His eyes lit up again. "Oh, me!"

We both laughed and headed to the kitchen, our bond stronger than ever.

Later that night I smiled as my husband eagerly dug into the chicken tetrazzini I had prepared for dinner. The savory, cheesy dish was one of his favorites, and his reaction reinforced the power of positive reinforcement. With each bite, I could see his appreciation and satisfaction. This was husband training at its finest. Much more effective than milk bonz.

As we finished up our meal, I decided it was time to wrap up this chapter on the fundamentals of training. "Well, I'd say that was a very successful lesson, wouldn't you?" I asked my husband.

He nodded enthusiastically. "Absolutely. I can really see how important patience, laughter, and positive reinforcement are for helping me be the best partner I can be."

"Wonderful. Then you understand why those are the core tools we'll be using as we move forward," I said.

I could tell by the determined glint in his eye that he was committed to this process. We had come a long way already.

"In the next chapter, we'll start working on some more advanced techniques to take your training to the next level," I explained. "We'll get into areas like communication, household responsibilities, and even intimacy skills."

At the mention of intimacy, I noticed my husband's cheeks flush slightly. But he also had a little grin turning up the corners of his mouth.

"That sounds…educational," he said with a wink.

"Oh, it will be," I assured him, returning the flirtatious look. The fun was just beginning.

With the fundamentals now firmly established, we were ready for the next exciting phase of our journey. And I had a feeling it would bring us even closer together.

Chapter 3

Basic Commands for Beginners

Forging on we continue exploring the exciting world of Husband Training, where dreams of a toilet seat perpetually in the down position can become reality! Say goodbye to those rude midnight wake-up calls of falling into the icy waters of an open toilet bowl. We're here to transform lackadaisical husbands into domestic warriors who instinctively put the seat down without being asked. Sound impossible? Not with our patented 'Pavlov's Potty' training technique!

Before we begin, let me tell you about the time my sister-in-law Sue took an unfortunate middle-of-the-night tumble into the toilet. Poor Sue was half-asleep when nature called at 3am. Still groggy, she plopped down on the toilet and got a rude awakening - literally! Sue's screams echoed through the house as she thrashed around in the freezing water. Her husband Carl came running into the bathroom, flipped the light on, and tried valiantly to pull her out while stifling laughter. Needless to say, Sue didn't find it nearly as funny as Carl did.

Moments like Sue's are exactly why learning the 'Put the Toilet Seat Down' command should be Priority #1 in your husband training curriculum. Follow these steps to ingrain this essential habit...

First, start by gently reminding your husband to put the seat down after he uses the bathroom. Say something like "Honey, could you please put the toilet seat back down when you're done? I'd really appreciate it." Make the request sweetly and without confrontation. If he forgets a few times, don't get upset - stay positive.

After a few days of polite reminders, it's time to get creative. Leave Post-It notes on the bathroom mirror saying things like "The toilet seat misses you!" or "Don't forget me!" You can also tape a humorous sign on the wall near the toilet reminding him to put the seat down. Search online for funny graphics or get crafty and make your own.

The next phase is reinforcing the habit through praise. Every time your husband remembers to put the seat down, shower him with positive feedback. Say things like "Thank you for putting the seat down, that was so thoughtful!" or give him a high-five. You can even create a sticker chart and give him a gold star each time he remembers. The positive reinforcement will motivate him to keep up the habit.

If your husband still seems to "forget" regularly, it's time to break out the secret weapon - the old fake rubber snake in the toilet trick. After he leaves the seat up, place the realistic looking snake in the bowl. When he goes to use the bathroom next and lifts the lid, he'll get the scare of his life! This should only be done occasionally, but it's a fun way to remind him in a humorous way. The snake prank will make the message stick. Just be prepared to console your frightened husband and to clean up all messes afterward!

With these tried-and-true techniques, the "Put the Toilet Seat Down" command will quickly become second nature. Consistency, creativity and positive reinforcement are key. In no time, you'll have a husband who instinctively puts that seat down every time without even thinking about it!

Sally stared despairingly into the open dishwasher, confronted yet again by a sight that made her blood boil - a fully loaded dishwasher, dishes stacked high, that her husband Tom had failed to load properly. This was not the first time, nor would it be the last, that Tom's inability to complete this simple household task had left Sally frustrated and furious. But she was determined that today would be the day it ended. She was going to train Tom, once and for all, in the fine art of loading the dishwasher.

First, she gathered the necessary supplies - a stack of plates, bowls, cups and cutlery. She beckoned Tom into the kitchen. "Today's the day you finally learn how to do this properly," she announced. Sally demonstrated how to insert the dishes without dropping them, starting from the top shelf. "Stack the plates neatly so they don't slide around." Next, the bowls, cups and cutlery - "silverware goes in the slots, handle side down."

Tom watched, brow furrowed, as Sally carefully placed each item in its proper place. "Your turn," she said, handing him a plate. Tom fumbled, nearly dropping a bowl. "Careful!" Sally said. She had him try again, guiding his hands gently. Once he got the hang of it, Sally let him work through the dishwasher contents himself. "See, you're getting it!" she said as Tom correctly slotted in a knife.

After he finished, Sally inspected Tom's work. A few minor issues, but not bad for a first try. "Excellent job, honey!" she said, rewarding him with a kiss on the cheek. She knew it would take more practice before Tom became a dishwasher loading expert, but today's session was an important first step. Consistent training and positive reinforcement would turn this chore from frustration to habit. And with teamwork, they'd maintain a sparkling clean kitchen.

Sally smiled as she watched Tom empty the dishwasher once it was finished, pleased with his progress. There were still some areas for improvement though.

"Not bad, babe! But let me show you a little trick," Sally said. She took a plate from the bottom rack and pretended to toss it Frisbee-style towards the cupboard.

"Whoaaa!" Tom yelped, lunging to catch the plate before it hit the floor and shattered into pieces.

Sally chuckled. "Kidding! But you see what I mean? Gotta be extra careful with these fragile items."

Tom let out a nervous laugh, his heart still pounding from the near miss.

"And make sure you double check that stuff is clean before putting it away," Sally added. "Remember that time I grabbed a 'clean' glass that still had ketchup smeared inside?"

Tom grimaced at the memory. "Ugh, yes. Not my finest moment."

"Hey, we all make mistakes," Sally said. "Like when I accidentally hit the door release and soaked the kitchen?"

They both laughed, the tension dissolving. Sally gave Tom another quick peck on the cheek. "You're doing great, babe. We'll turn you into a pro dishwasher loader/emptier in no time!"

Tom smiled and pulled Sally in for a proper kiss. "Thanks for training me. I know it'll take some work, but we make a pretty good team."

"Alright, time for the next lesson," Sally said, leading Tom by the hand into the bedroom. "I know you're eager to get to the good stuff, but we gotta have a little chat first."

Tom plopped down on the edge of the bed. "Oh boy, this sounds serious."

"It is serious!" Sally said, hands on her hips. "This is about Dutch ovens."

Tom looked puzzled. "You wanna cook some stew before we fool around?"

Sally rolled her eyes. "No, not those kinds of Dutch ovens. I'm talking about when someone farts under the covers and then holds the other person's head under, so they have to smell it."

"Ohhh," Tom said, laughing. "Yeah, those are pretty hilarious."

"It's not hilarious - it's toxic!" Sally said. "So, no more trying to 'Dutch oven' me during foreplay, got it?"

Tom held up his hands. "Hey, just admit you loved it!"

"I'm not laughing Tom," Sally said, glaring at him.

"Okay, okay, I'm sorry," Tom said sincerely with his fingers crossed behind his back. "No more Dutch ovens - I promise."

(Note* This is an area where your husband might need additional positive reinforcement to break the natural male instinct. You may have to employ the shock collar on one or more occasions.)

Sally's expression softened. "Good. Now come over here and let's get back to more pleasant activities," she said with a wink.

Tom grinned and pulled Sally down onto the bed. They kissed passionately, ready to enjoy some stink-free foreplay at last.

Sally broke off the kiss and sat up, a serious look on her face again.

"There is one more thing," she said. "Remember that night last month when you had chili for dinner?"

Tom grinned. "Uhh, kinda hard to forget that one."

"I still have nightmares!" Sally exclaimed. "It was like you had a rotting garbage dump coming out of your butt. I had to sleep in the bathroom just to escape the toxic fumes."

"Sorry, babe," Tom said sheepishly. "I did warn you it was three alarm chili."

"I almost had to go to the hospital to get my stomach pumped and nasal passages irrigated," Sally said dramatically. "It was that bad."

Tom tried not to laugh. "Wow, really? I didn't think it was hospital worthy."

"I'm dead serious," Sally said, narrowing her eyes. "I couldn't breathe, I was so nauseous. You're just lucky I didn't smother you with a pillow in your sleep."

"Some of my fondest memories of camping trips with the scouts started out with that chili," Tom said.

"I'm making that an official rule," Sally declared. "No chili or other gas-inducing foods before bedtime."

"Yes ma'am," Tom said with a mock salute. "Now, can we get back to the good stuff? I promise no Dutch ovens or toxic gas leaks tonight."

"You better not," Sally said, a smile finally breaking through. She pulled Tom close, and they picked up where they'd left off, savoring an evening of stink-free passion at last.

"Ah, that's better," Sally sighed contentedly afterward, as they lay tangled in each other's arms.

"Mmm hmm," Tom murmured in agreement, running his fingers lazily through her hair.

"It's amazing what a little communication and compromise can do for a relationship," Sally mused.

"You're telling me," Tom said. "Who knew all our bedroom woes could be solved by a simple 'no chili before sex' rule?"

"Right? It's almost like having a well-trained husband," Sally teased.

"Hey now, I'm not a dog you can teach tricks to," Tom objected playfully.

"No, not at all," Sally said, kissing his cheek. "A well-trained husband is more like a unicorn - rare and magical."

Tom grinned. "I can live with that comparison."

"And we're just getting started, mister," Sally added with a wink. "Next up, we tackle the thorny subject of you actually remembering important dates without me having to remind you a thousand times."

Tom groaned jokingly. "Baby steps, baby! I'm still working on the putting the toilet seat down thing."

Sally laughed and snuggled against his chest. "Don't worry, we've got time..."

Chapter 4

Advanced Techniques for Husband Mastery

"Listen up, maggots! Today we'll be whipping you sorry saps into shape with our Remembering Important Dates Bootcamp! Many of you worthless worms couldn't remember your anniversary if your life depended on it. Well, guess what? Around here, it does!

First technique: Check Yourself Before You Wreck Yourself! Wives, print out calendars for the whole year and tape them everywhere your hopeless hubby looks—the bathroom mirror, the fridge, his car dashboard. Circle every birthday, anniversary, and special event in threatening red ink. That'll drill it into his tiny brain!

Second technique: Pavlov's Dogs Have Nothing on You! Condition your husband with rewards and punishments. If he forgets, make him sleep on the couch. If he remembers, reward him with his favorite meal. He'll beg for your meatloaf in no time!

Now drop and give me 20! This bootcamp isn't over until you lugs can recite your anniversary date in your sleep! Hup to it!"

"Alright ladies, time for a real-life example of what happens when your man fails to remember an important date. Let me tell you about my buddy Larry and the time he forgot his 10th anniversary.

Poor Larry spent weeks preparing to surprise his wife Jenny with a trip to Hawaii for their big milestone. He booked the flights, made the hotel reservations, even bought some new Tommy Bahama shirts to wear on the beach. Larry was feeling pretty proud of himself.

The big day finally arrived, and Larry woke up before Jenny, excited to reveal his amazing gift over breakfast in bed. But when Jenny rolled over with tears in her eyes and said, 'I can't believe you forgot our anniversary,' Larry's heart sank.

Turns out, while he nailed the trip planning, he forgot to wish Jenny a happy anniversary or get her a gift on the real day, a week before the Hawaii trip. Larry tried apologizing and showing her the printed itinerary, but Jenny wasn't having it. She kicked him out of bed and made him sleep on the couch for a week, Hawaii plans be damned.

Larry learned the hard way that grand gestures don't replace acknowledging the actual anniversary date. Husbands! - Don't be a Larry! Mark your calendars and set phone reminders, or you'll end up in the doghouse too."

As Larry's fiasco shows, remembering important dates is a crucial skill for any husband! Coming up in the Listening Without Fixing Workshop, we'll explore how to really hear what she's saying, instead of trying to solve all her problems.

Jenny came home that evening, exhausted after a stressful day at the office. She collapsed onto the couch with a groan.

"Rough day, huh?" said Larry sympathetically.

"The worst," complained Jenny. "My boss rejected my proposal, I got yelled at by a client, and I spilled coffee all over my favorite blouse." She gestured at the stain on her shirt.

"Wow, sounds awful," said Larry. His mind was already whirring with solutions. "Maybe you could ask your boss to reconsider the proposal. And we can take your blouse to the dry cleaners. As for the client, just remember you can't please everyone..."

Jenny held up her hand. "Larry. Please. I don't need you to fix all my problems right now. I just need you to listen."

Larry blinked in surprise. "Oh. Sorry, honey." He sat down next to Jenny. "Tell me more about this terrible day of yours."

Jenny sighed. "I just wish my boss valued my ideas more. And that client had no right to be so rude! I tried so hard on that proposal..." She trailed off, looking dejected.

Larry resisted the urge to jump in with reassurances and solutions. Instead, he just nodded sympathetically. "That all sounds so frustrating. I'm sorry they didn't see your value today."

Jenny gave him a small smile. "Thanks, babe. That actually makes me feel a little better."

Larry smiled back, relieved. Maybe he was getting the hang of this whole listening thing after all.

Jenny patted Larry on the knee. "You know, I really appreciate you just listening tonight. I know it's not easy for you to sit still when you hear about a problem."

Larry chuckled. "Well, I can't say my mind didn't start spinning with ways to make it all better. But I'm trying to get better at just being present for you."

"And I love you for it," said Jenny. She leaned over and gave him a quick kiss.

Larry grinned goofily. For a moment he basked in the glow of being an attentive husband.

Then Jenny hopped up from the couch. "Okay, enough wallowing for me. Time to move on to more pleasant things." She clapped her hands together. "Like our next training exercise - the Finding Lost Items Treasure Hunt!"

Larry groaned. "Do we have to? You know I hate trying to find stuff."

"Yes, we do!" said Jenny brightly. "It's time you learn once and for all not to just throw your things around the house then ask me to find them for you."

She grabbed a notepad and pen from the coffee table. "Here's how it works..."

Jenny tapped her pen against the notepad. "First, I'll hide 5 or 6 of your most commonly misplaced items around the house. Your keys, wallet, glasses, TV remote, etc. Then I'll leave clues leading you to each item, like a treasure hunt!"

She scribbled on the pad. "Ooh, maybe the theme could be pirate treasure, and I'll draw little maps as the clues!"

Larry rubbed his forehead. "Do we really have to make it so complicated? Can't I just look around for the stuff like normal?"

"Nope!" said Jenny. "It has to be fun, or you won't learn. Now let me hide these things..."

She grabbed the TV remote, Larry's glasses, and a few other items and scurried around the house. Larry heard small thuds and the squeak of furniture as she wedged his belongings in silly spots.

"Okay, ready!" Jenny returned with a grin. In a pirate voice she announced "Here's yer first clue, matey!" and handed Larry a crude map.

He sighed and followed its directions to the kitchen. The remote was sitting in the freezer.

Next the map led him outside to the grill, where his wallet was cooking alongside the burger patties.

After finding his keys in the bathroom sink and his watch under the rug, Larry had to admit he was starting to enjoy himself. There was something satisfying about the hunt.

Jenny smiled as Larry proudly showed her each discovered item. "You're learning already! Pretty soon you'll be stashing your things properly on your own."

Larry had to agree. Maybe methodically hiding his everyday items all over the house wasn't such a crazy idea after all - if he didn't have to move anything to look for them. That would be a deal breaker!

Larry reflected on the afternoon's activities as he sank into his favorite armchair, newly reunited with the TV remote. Though unorthodox, Jenny's treasure hunt method had been oddly effective. He could already feel his memory improving as his brain subconsciously catalogued all the new hiding spots.

Jenny curled up next to him on the couch. "Not bad for your first hunt, babe. Just think of all the time we'll save not looking for lost stuff. Now you can spend that energy remembering important things instead…like anniversary dates!"

She elbowed him playfully in the ribs. Larry chuckled. Her unconventional techniques may have seemed silly at first, but he couldn't argue with the results.

"You know, you're right honey. I guess I should be more open-minded about your unique approach to keeping me in line. Lord knows I need it!"

Jenny smiled and gave him a peck on the cheek. "That's the spirit! We make a pretty good team."

Larry nodded. With Jenny's creativity and persistence balanced by his willingness to try new things, they could overcome any marital challenge - with humor and love. He took her hand gratefully, excited to see what she'd come up with next in her unorthodox crusade to create the perfect husband.

Chapter 5

The Playful Approach to Problem Solving

I bolted upright in bed, my heart pounding as I scanned the dark room. Had I heard something? A faint clattering sound echoed from the kitchen down the hall. I glanced at my wife sleeping soundly beside me and slowly slid out from under the covers. Padding softly across the room, I eased open the door and peered into the hallway. More noises drifted from the kitchen - the fridge opening, cupboards gently closing. An intruder? My pulse raced as I crept toward the sounds, wishing I had something more than my bathrobe to defend myself with.

Rounding the corner, I flipped on the light switch, ready to confront the thief. "Aha!" I yelled triumphantly. But there was no menacing figure rifling through our shelves. Only my wife, frozen with a jar of mayonnaise in one hand and my toothpaste tube in the other, her pillow imposter, upstairs in the bed strategically placed under the blankets. She burst out laughing.

"You should see your face!" she howled. "I got you good this time!"

I shook my head, torn between exasperation and amusement. My wife's prank wars were infamous. Last month I'd retaliated by putting confetti in the showerhead.

"Okay, you win this round," I chuckled. "But remember - prank wars need rules. Nothing that causes real harm or hurt feelings."

She nodded, eyes still dancing with mirth. "Of course. All in good fun."

I gave her a quick kiss on the cheek. "Truce for now. But you'd better watch your back!" I called over my shoulder as I headed back to bed, smiling to myself. Her pranks may drive me crazy, but they kept our relationship lively. Still, I'd have to start planning my counterattack soon...

The next morning, I sat at my desk plotting my revenge. My wife's toothpaste-mayo swap gave me some ideas. I scribbled down a list of potential pranks:

- Fill her car with balloons so they avalanche out when she opens the door.

- Cover her office desk in sticky notes.

- Put a rubber band around the sink sprayer so she gets soaked when she turns on the faucet.

- Replace her shampoo with hair dye so she ends up with green locks.

I chuckled evilly, imagining her reactions. Timing and secrecy would be key. I'd need to enlist help to pull off the car prank. Maybe I could get her brother involved - he'd love messing with his sister.

As I schemed, I glanced at a photo of us laughing together on our wedding day. Pranks brought out her spirited side, which was one of the things I loved most about her.

I headed to the store, whistling cheerfully as I stocked up on supplies. I sent a quick text to her brother: "Epic prank war underway. I'll need your help with Operation Balloon Bomb..."

This meant war! But it would be the fun, bonding kind that brought us closer together. I could already imagine us watching the balloon video and cracking up for years to come. Maybe I'd even have a viral hit for my retirement fund. Humor glued our relationship together. I couldn't wait to make my wife laugh again!

I rolled my eyes as he did his silly voice impression during our argument about how to load the dishwasher.

"It goes cups first, then plates, then bowls!" he said in a goofy, high-pitched tone.

Despite herself, she chuckled. "No way! Bowls on the bottom, then plates, then cups on top," she responded, mimicking a pirate voice.

Our voices got increasingly ridiculous as we debated the proper dishwasher packing technique. Pretty soon we both dissolved into laughter, the tension diffused.

Later, when we argued about how to pronounce "tomato," I exaggeratedly enunciated "toe-MAY-toe" in my best Shakespearean actor voice. He cracked up and declared "tuh-MAH-toe" in an equally dramatic fashion.

We playfully bickered, neither giving in, but the humor made it impossible to stay mad. I loved that we could poke fun during disagreements instead of letting them escalate. Laughter brought us closer.

The key was maintaining mutual respect while injecting comedy. I never used hurtful sarcasm or mean jokes. The goal was to lighten the mood, not put him down. If we avoided insults, humor could strengthen our bond.

I decided it was time to turn our boring chores into hilarious comedy acts. As I vacuumed, I belted out showtunes and danced with the vacuum cleaner like it was my dance partner. My husband doubled over laughing as I dramatically lip synced and twirled around the living room.

When it was his turn to do laundry, he grabbed a laundry basket and pretended it was his guitar, rocking out to air guitar solos while tossing clothes into the washing machine. I cheered and whistled like his "audience."

We came up with choreographed dance routines while cleaning the bathroom, complete with dramatic leaps across the tile floors. The wacky moves made scrubbing toilets and sinks much more fun.

During dishwashing, we took turns doing play-by-play commentary like sportscasters, narrating each plate and utensil as we washed it. Our exaggerated announcer voices and running commentary turned a boring task into an evening of entertainment.

No matter how silly we got, the key was maintaining a spirit of teamwork and never mocking each other's comedy attempts. Our goal was laughter, not criticism. Bringing humor into chores gave us quality bonding time instead of drudgery. I loved that we could be ridiculous together. Laughter made everything better.

I smiled as I watched my husband grab the mop and start gliding across the kitchen floor as if ice skating. He twirled and leapt, the mop propelling him into not so graceful arcs. His exaggerated facial expressions of concentration made me chuckle.

"And next up is Michael Spinmop performing a routine he calls 'Dancing with the Dirt'," I announced in my best announcer voice.

Michael curtsied and continued his choreographed mop dance, using the mop handle to strike poses and pointing his toes in time with the music.

When he finished with a triple spin and a bow, I jumped up applauding. "The judges are sure to award Michael a perfect score for that amazing performance!"

Michael laughed and tossed me the mop. "Alright, it's your turn now. Let's see what you've got!"

I knew I couldn't match his grace, so I decided to go for humor instead. Gripping the mop handle, I launched into an air guitar riff, headbanging wildly. As I "shredded" up and down the mop neck, I leapt onto the kitchen table, ignoring Michael's horrified expression.

"Get down from there!" he yelled over my guitar solo wailing.

I jumped down and dropped to my knees for the big finish, sliding across the freshly mopped floor in my socks. I struck a final rock star pose, breathing hard.

Michael tried to look disapproving but couldn't help cracking up. "You're cleaning that floor again, you know," he said, shaking his head.

"Worth it!" I laughed, pulling him in for a kiss.

"Alright Dancing Queen, as fun as that was, we still have more cleaning to do."

He nodded, catching his breath. As amusing as our choreographed mop routines were, the floors weren't going to scrub themselves.

We moved on to the bathrooms, armed with sprays, scrubs, and our secret weapon - a Bluetooth speaker. As an upbeat playlist filled the room, we sang and danced our way through the grimy grout and mildew-lined tiles.

Michael belted out a hairbrush rendition of "Dancing Queen" while attacking the tub. I joined in with a mop microphone as we laughed and twirled around each other.

By the time we hit the final chorus, the bathroom was sparkling. We collapsed against each other, giggling at our antics.

"This was way more fun than just silently scrubbing away," Michael remarked.

I nodded in agreement. "Who knew chores could turn into such great bonding time?"

It was true. Taking a humorous approach transformed our tedious tasks into shared experiences that brought us closer together. With laughter, teamwork, and a touch of creativity, even the most mundane chores became enjoyable.

As we moved on to tackle the next cleaning project, I was reminded of the transformative power of humor. When faced with any disagreeable task, whether chores or bigger relationship challenges, a playful, lighthearted mindset can make all the difference. Approached together, with compassion and good humor, any problem can become an opportunity for joy and connection.

Chapter 6

The Great Outdoors: Husbands in the Wild

The fluorescent lights of the department store glared down on me as I perused the clearance rack, my husband Michael trailing behind like a sullen teenager. I held up a blue sweater for his inspection. "How about this one?"

Michael barely glanced at it before shaking his head. "I don't know. Can we go soon?"

I sighed, returning the sweater to the rack. My husband's legendary aversion to shopping had struck again. Most husbands got bored browsing the racks, impatiently checking their watches as their wives compared fabrics and hem lengths. But Michael took it to another level. Mere minutes into any shopping trip, he was shuffling his feet, looking for escape routes like a prisoner planning a jailbreak.

I grabbed another top, a red blouse with ruffles. "What do you think of this?" I asked brightly, determined to find at least one item before Michael's eyes glazed over completely.

He scrunched his nose. "Too frilly. Are you almost done?"

"Almost," I lied. In truth, we'd only been there twenty minutes. I had at least three more departments to check.

Michael sighed, eyeing a display of men's watches. I could almost see the countdown starting in his head. My husband's distaste for shopping was legendary among our couple friends. While most wives only had to endure minor grumbling during trips to the mall, I got full-on mutiny. I couldn't take Michael anywhere with more than two aisles without him trying to gnaw his own arm off to escape.

I knew I had to move fast before he staged a sit-in protest right there in the women's section. I grabbed three more items at random and made a beeline for the checkout, Michael following dutifully behind, his relief evident. Sure, it meant I rarely got to shop at a leisurely pace. But at least I still had all my limbs intact. For now, anyway.

I breathed a sigh of relief as we walked out of the department store, my hurried purchases in hand. But I knew the real test was yet to come - making it through to Sunday dinner with my family without Michael turning the table over in a fit of boredom induced rage.

My husband has many fine qualities, but patience during extended family gatherings is not one of them. Between my mother's overbearing questions, my brother's tasteless jokes, and my great aunt's tendency to pinch cheeks, Michael is ready to tear his hair out after just fifteen minutes.

As we pulled up to my parents' house, I turned to Michael with an encouraging smile. "Just think of it as a highly interactive trip to the museum exhibits of eccentric relatives," I said.

Michael grunted, his version of amused agreement.

No sooner had we stepped inside than the onslaught began. My mother enveloped me in a hug, immediately asking why I'd cut my hair and if I was eating enough. My brother made a crude joke about Michael's receding hairline. And Great Aunt Edna went straight for Michael's cheek with her pointy red nails.

Michael shot me a pained look, but I just smiled sympathetically. We had a long road ahead, but at least it would be entertaining. I made a mental note to stop for ice cream on the way home. Michael was going to need it after surviving this three-ring family circus.

Michael's eye started twitching as my mother launched into the details of her menopause. I could see him scanning the room for an escape route, so I jumped in.

"Hey Michael, why don't you come help me get some appetizers from the kitchen?" I said brightly, linking my arm through his and steering him away.

In the kitchen, I grabbed a tray of cheese and crackers. "Here, have some emergency rations," I said, handing him a stack of crackers piled high with brie.

He shoved them in his mouth gratefully. "This is brutal," he mumbled through a mouthful of cheese. "Your family is like a pack of wolves."

I laughed. "I know, I'm sorry. But we can get through this together." I squeezed his hand supportively. "Just stick with me and we'll employ some diversionary tactics as needed."

Michael nodded, gearing up for round two.

We headed back out to find my great uncle Murray in full swing talking about his gallbladder surgery. Tom's eyes glazed over. I made eye contact with my brother across the room, silently pleading for help.

Taking the cue, my brother interrupted Uncle Murray. "Hey! Who wants to see some pictures from my trip to Iceland?" he announced loudly. The relatives clustered around eagerly, giving Michael a much-needed break.

He smiled gratefully at me, and I winked. We were surviving by utilizing every resource and ally possible. And despite the chaos, or maybe because of it, I was filled with immense love for my eccentric, exasperating family. As long as Michael and I stuck together, we could handle anything. Even the dreaded family reunion.

"Alright, here are a few more tips for maintaining your sanity," I said, turning to Michael.

"First, schedule regular breaks from the family fray. Whether it's a quick walk around the block or retreating to a quiet corner of the house, stepping away briefly will give you a chance to catch your breath."

Michael nodded. "Good call. I could use some fresh air after Murray's gallbladder story."

I laughed. "Exactly. Second tip - find some common ground with even the most challenging relatives. Compliment Aunt Janice's terrible casserole or ask Uncle Leo about his stamp collection. Making small connections can go a long way."

"Got it. Find common ground," he said.

"Lastly, embrace the madness," I continued. "Accept that awkward moments and mishaps are inevitable at big family events. Being able to laugh at the chaos will keep you from losing your mind."

I smiled and squeezed Michael's hand again. "Stay flexible, stick together, and we'll get through this nuttiness no problem."

Michael smiled back. "Thanks for the tips. With you by my side, I feel ready for anything your family can throw at me."

Arm in arm, we headed back to rejoin the festivities, united in our quest to survive and find humor amidst the family reunion madness.

"Well, we survived the family reunion hurricane," I said to my husband as we collapsed onto the couch back home. "Now it's time for our long-awaited vacation!"

Michael nodded wearily. "I'm so ready to relax after that weekend."

"Me too," I said. "Having a well-trained partner like you makes vacation planning so much easier."

Michael smiled proudly. "All that husband training is really paying off."

"You were so helpful researching activities, booking flights and hotels, and creating an itinerary," I continued.

"Of course, vacations never go quite according to plan," Michael replied knowingly.

"Right, we have to be ready for the unexpected!" I said. "Like the time we got on the wrong train in Prague and ended up in a tiny village with no idea how to get back."

Michael laughed. "Or when I got pickpocketed in Barcelona and we had to go to the consulate to replace my passport."

"Don't forget about the tropical storm that rerouted our cruise to Jamaica instead of the Bahamas," I added.

We smiled thinking back on past travel mishaps.

"With you by my side, I know we can handle whatever adventures come our way," Michael said, taking my hand.

"Exactly!" I squeezed his hand excitedly. "As long as we stick together and keep laughing, it will be an unforgettable trip."

Ready for new stories and memories, we headed off on our next vacation together. I was secretly just hoping he didn't pee on the outside wall of the Louvre.

"Even when things go awry, having a sense of humor and being flexible are key to surviving vacation catastrophes," I explained.

Michael nodded in agreement. "Like when we got food poisoning in Mexico. I'll never forget you still trying to salsa dance despite running to the bathroom every 10 minutes."

We laughed at the memory.

"Or when the airline lost our luggage on the way to Hawaii and we had to wear flower shirts from the gift shop for 3 days straight," he added.

"We really do make the best of unfortunate situations," I said. "As they say, 'When life hands you lemons, make lemonade!'"

Michael smiled. "Your positivity and spontaneity make every vacation an adventure."

"And your patience and problem-solving skills get us out of any sticky situation," I countered.

"I guess that's why we make such a great team," he said.

"Absolutely," I agreed. "But it's also important that we communicate and compromise when planning vacations together."

Michael nodded. "Like finding a balance between relaxing beach days and action-packed excursions."

"Right, we have to make sure both our needs are met," I said. "Maybe we alternate who gets to choose the activities each day."

"Perfect. When we're together, any vacation is a dream," he replied happily.

With open minds, senses of humor, and eagerness for adventure, we set off on our next sojourn as an unstoppable vacation team.

"Well, that concludes navigating life's adventures with your partner," I said. "We've covered the wild rides of shopping, surviving family gatherings, and vacationing together."

Michael chuckled. "It's been a journey, but I feel fully trained and ready for anything."

"I'm so glad to hear that!" I replied. "Just remember, with a little patience, compromise, and humor, you can handle any situation life throws your way."

Michael smiled and nodded in agreement.

"Now, let's move on to the next exercise" I continued enthusiastically. "Get ready to learn the secrets of maintaining a happy and healthy relationship through the ups and downs of life. We'll cover communication strategies, ideas for keeping the spark alive, and more. You won't want to miss this!"

I smiled at Michael warmly. "Well dear, ready to turn the page with me?"

Michael squeezed my hand affectionately. "Absolutely! I can't wait to keep learning and growing in this relationship together."

And with bright eyes and light hearts, we embarked on the next leg of our never-ending journey toward the holy grail - marital bliss.

Chapter 7

Beyond Husband Training

There's a loud crash as dishes shatter on the kitchen floor. Sally stands surrounded by broken shards, clutching a plate in each hand.

"Whoops," she says, glancing sheepishly at her husband John. "Looks like we're having paper plates tonight."

John shakes his head and chuckles. "Or we could order takeout?"

Sally laughs. "Good thinking. My cooking isn't worth this mess anyway."

She drops the remaining plates on the counter with a clatter and steps gingerly through the wreckage to grab the broom. As she sweeps, John opens a drawer and rummages for a takeout menu.

"Wonder what caused you to drop them in the first place?" he asks.

"Oh, I was just thinking about how much I hate doing the dishes," Sally says. "I guess I got a little careless."

John grins. "Say no more. I hereby decree that I will handle all dish duties from now on."

"My hero!" Sally swoons theatrically. She dumps the shards into the trash and leans the broom against the fridge.

"In all seriousness though," she says, "little moments like these remind me not to take things too seriously. Who cares about a few broken plates? We still have each other."

She steps closer and squeezes John's hand affectionately. He pulls her into an embrace.

"You're right," he says. "As long as we can laugh together, we can survive anything life throws our way."

Sally smiles at him. "Even my terrible cooking."

They share a tender kiss amidst the chaos of their kitchen.

John pulls away from the kiss and grins down at Sally.

"Speaking of laughter, I've got an idea," he says. "Why don't we have a comedy night once a week? We can make popcorn, get comfy on the couch, and watch some of our favorite funny movies or shows."

Sally's eyes light up. "That sounds amazing! We definitely need more laughter in our lives."

She starts mentally scrolling through all the hilarious movies and TV shows they could watch together.

"Ooh, we could start with that new season of that show we love," she suggests excitedly. "Or rewatch some of our favorite rom coms!"

John nods, grabbing his phone to look up comedy specials and funny viral videos they can add to their watchlist.

"And we should send each other memes and jokes throughout the week too," he says. "Laughter medicine for the soul."

"I love that," Sally says. She pulls out her own phone, quickly forwarding John a funny meme she saw earlier that day.

John laughs out loud when he opens it. "See, this is perfect!" he says. "With little moments of humor like this sprinkled in each day, we'll be able to handle anything life throws at us."

Sally smiles and squeezes his hand in agreement. John is almost fully trained, and she didn't have to use the shock collar more than one time!

No matter what stresses or conflicts arise, they resolve to keep laughter and lightheartedness flowing freely in their relationship. With a weekly comedy night to look forward to, and funny memes filling their phones, they feel certain their love can weather any storm, as long as they face it with a smile.

John smiles as he thinks back on their journey together so far.

"Remember our first vacation to the beach house?" he asks Sally. "When that huge thunderstorm rolled in and knocked the power out?"

Sally chuckles and nods. "We were so annoyed at first, with no electricity or Wi-Fi!"

"But then we started goofing around to pass the time," John continues. "You grabbed two flashlights and held them under your face to make a scary ghost costume."

"And you used the deck furniture to build an indoor mini golf course!" Sally says, laughing at the memory.

"We ended up having so much fun that night just being silly and laughing together," John says warmly. "It's one of my favorite memories."

Sally squeezes his hand again. "Mine too," she agrees. "We definitely didn't take that situation too seriously. And our ability to laugh and play together got us through it."

John nods. "No matter what life throws at us - big or small - if we can keep laughing, we'll be just fine."

Sally smiles. As they reminisce on the humor and playfulness that has always been a part of their love, she feels grateful for the hilarity of their journey together so far. With laughter lighting their way, she knows their future holds nothing but joy.

"You know, that gives me an idea for how we can celebrate our upcoming anniversary," John says. "Why don't we plan a fun night recreating some of our favorite funny memories?"

Sally's eyes light up. "That sounds amazing! We could decorate the house like during that beach trip - string up some twinkle lights, light candles and build that mini golf course in the living room."

"And we can dig out those old scrapbooks and photo albums to reminisce on all the hilarious moments we've shared over the years," John adds.

"Ooh, and let's dress up in some of our old ridiculous outfits, like my ghost costume!" Sally says excitedly.

John laughs. "I love it. It'll be a night filled with laughter and celebration of all the joy we've experienced together."

"Speaking of joyful celebrations..." Sally says, "I have another idea for a funny gift we can exchange. How about we each make a personalized joke book for the other, filled with inside jokes, funny memories and custom illustrations?"

John grins. "That's brilliant! I can't wait to come up with silly cartoons and poems referencing things only you would understand."

"And I'll make sure to include some of your famous dad jokes and puns," Sally teases.

John chuckles. "Well, I know my gift to you will bring lots of laughs and smiles. Here's to celebrating the hilarity of our love in creative, meaningful ways."

Sally leans over and kisses his cheek.

With laughter and playfulness woven into their relationship, Sally and John continue brainstorming humorous ideas to commemorate their milestones, embracing the lighthearted spirit that has always defined their hilarious love story.

Sally sighs contentedly as she snuggles into John's embrace on the couch. "You know, as much as we joke around, I'm so thankful for our ability to laugh together. It really takes the stress out of life's challenges."

John nods, running his fingers through her hair. "Absolutely. I don't know how I'd get through tough times without your sense of humor lifting my spirits."

"And just being able to be silly and let loose with each other creates such joy and intimacy between us," Sally adds.

"Right," John agrees. "Sharing laughter strengthens our bond in a really special way. It's like we have this whole secret world of inside jokes and funny memories."

Sally grins at him. "Exactly! No matter what happens, I know I can always count on you to make me smile."

John kisses the top of her head. "You do the same for me, babe."

A peaceful silence settles between them as they reflect on the lighthearted atmosphere humor provides in their relationship. Sally feels deeply grateful for their ability to face life's ups and downs with laughter and levity.

After a few moments, John clears his throat. "Well, I guess we should move onto the next lesson about being the best partner we can be in this marriage."

Sally nods, sitting up. "Yes, it's so important we keep working to improve ourselves individually and as a couple."

As they transition into discussing personal growth and commitment, Sally and John cherish the joy humor brings into their relationship, helping create a positive foundation. With laughter, intimacy, and dedication, they're determined to build a marriage that celebrates the hilarious and heartwarming moments life brings.

John turns to Sally, taking her hands in his. "I think one of the best things we can do is really listen to each other. Like when you tell me about your day, I should give you my full attention instead of just pretending to listen while I scroll on my phone."

Sally smiles and nods. "Definitely. And I could be better about not interrupting you when you're talking. Active listening shows we truly care."

"Expressing more gratitude is important too," John adds. "I want to get better at thanking you for even the small stuff, like making dinner or doing the laundry. I'm thankful for you every day."

Sally's eyes well up. "Aww, me too. And I want to be more aware of showing empathy when you're stressed from work. Taking time to understand where you're coming from makes a big difference."

John pulls Sally in for a hug. As they hold each other, he says, "This journey of growth together never ends. We gotta keep learning and adapting to each phase of our marriage."

Sally looks up at John. "You're so right. Reading relationship books, going to workshops, even trying couples counseling could help us gain new tools to deepen our bond."

John caresses Sally's cheek. "As long as we're committed to working on ourselves and this marriage, I know our love will only grow stronger."

Sally's eyes shine. "I know it too. We got this!" She seals her words with a kiss.

John looks into Sally's eyes and says, "This journey we're on together has had plenty of ups and downs. But the laughter we share, the way we celebrate each milestone, and the personal growth we strive for - those are the keys to a marriage that can weather any storm."

Sally nods, "So true. Our commitment to humor, love and learning makes this relationship fulfilling in a way I never could have imagined."

John smiles, "No matter what life throws at us, we'll get through it stronger if we hold onto joy, romance and bettering ourselves." He pulls Sally close. "I wouldn't want to walk this road with anyone but you."

John closes the book and sets it on the nightstand. He turns to Sally and says, "Well, I don't know about you, but I'm excited to dive into the next lesson tomorrow night."

Sally grins. "Oh definitely! It's about effective communication. I can't wait to learn ways we can understand each other even better."

John laughs, "With as much as we talk, improving communication will be a big win!" He clicks off the lamp as they snuggle into bed. Sally falls asleep dreaming of what new insights their relationship journey will reveal.

Sally wakes up the next morning feeling energized and optimistic about her marriage. Over breakfast, she tells John, "I had the best dream that we were communicating so clearly, we could read each other's minds!"

John chuckles, "Well, we may not develop psychic abilities from your training sessions, but I have no doubt we'll find ways to connect on an even deeper level."

Sally smiles and squeezes his hand affectionately. "You're right. I'm just eager to get to that next level!"

"Me too," John agrees. "But first, we have a busy day ahead of us. Are you ready to seize it with humor and joy?"

"Absolutely!" Sally replies. She plants a quick kiss on John's cheek before dancing out the door, excited by all the laughter and learning still to come on their journey together.

On the way out she notices a rancid smell, but she decides to let that one go, after all, training is a process and despite how proud she is of her husband, Rome wasn't built in a day, and they did have chili last night.

Chapter 8

The Graduation Ceremony

Assessing Your Husband's Progress:

The first rays of the morning sun crept through the blinds, assaulting my eyes like a drill sergeant blowing a whistle. I groaned and pulled the covers over my head, but it was too late - I was awake. Beside me, my husband snored loudly, dead to the world. Lucky for some.

I shoved him roughly. "Rise and shine, sleepyhead. Time for your morning assessment."

He grunted in protest, but eventually sat up, hair sticking out at all angles like a mad scientist. I clicked my pen and consulted my checklist. "Let's start with personal hygiene. Did you remember to clip your toenails this week?"

"Do we have to do this now?" he whined. "It's Saturday!"

I gave him a withering look. "Compliance is key. Now, toenail clipping - yes, or no?"

He sighed. "Yes, dear."

"Good. And did you floss every night like I've told you?" I asked.

"Yes, yes, I flossed," he said irritably.

I made a check mark on my paper. "Excellent. You're making progress." I patted his leg. "Now, time to get up. I'll expect you downstairs in ten minutes to start preparing breakfast."

He flopped back onto the bed with a dramatic groan. I smiled to myself as I headed to the bathroom. The training was proceeding perfectly.

I headed downstairs, humming to myself. The journey of husband training was well underway. When I first started this process, my husband was utterly hopeless - lazy, oblivious, completely dependent on me to manage our household. But through patience, persistence, and judicious use of positive and negative reinforcement, he became a real partner.

Of course, it hadn't been easy. There were plenty of bumps along the road where he resisted the new status quo. Like when I first required him to learn to cook. What a disaster those early meals were! Burnt, under seasoned, sometimes entirely inedible. I can still remember the time he tried to pass off charcoal briquettes as barbeque chicken.

But with time, even his cooking improved. Now his meals were…adequate, if not gourmet. And the look of pride on his face when I complimented him on a dish was priceless. It made all the frustration worth it.

I settled onto the couch with my morning coffee, listening to the sounds of whisking and sizzling coming from the kitchen. The results of my comedy-filled adventure in husband training were so gratifying. My once useless spouse was now a capable, contributing partner. Our relationship had grown stronger, our laughter louder, our bond deeper.

And this was just the beginning. As I sipped my coffee, I started planning the next phase of our journey together...

Here is a continuation of the scene focusing on the importance of love, laughter, and acceptance along with final words of wisdom and witty farewells:

My husband emerged from the kitchen holding two plates piled high with pancakes, eggs, and bacon.

"Breakfast is served, my queen," he said with an exaggerated bow.

I smiled at him. "Why thank you, kind sir. This looks wonderful."

We dug into our meal with gusto. The food was delicious - perfectly cooked and seasoned. My husband beamed at my compliments.

As we ate, I reflected on how far we'd come. The bumbling, incapable man I'd married was gone, replaced by this attentive, contributing partner. Our journey had been filled with laughter, but also tears, frustration, and many difficult conversations.

Yet we'd persevered, always remembering that at the core, there was deep love between us. All the coaching, nagging, and yes, humor, had simply been different means to nourish that love.

Now here we were, laughing together over breakfast on a sunny morning. The future stretched before us, filled with possibility. Our comedic adventure in husband training was ending, but our journey as partners was only beginning.

I reached out and squeezed his hand, meeting his eyes. "I know we still have so much to learn together. But I want you to know - I'm so proud of the man you've become. I can't wait to see what comes next for us."

He smiled, eyes glistening. "Me too, honey. We make a pretty great team."

I raised my coffee mug. "To the ongoing adventure of marriage, with equal parts wisdom, wit, and love."

We clinked mugs. The rest of our lives awaited, filled with laughter, growth, and joyful togetherness. This husband training comedy had a happy ending after all.

Appendix 1: Husband Training Worksheets and Exercises

"Whew, we covered a lot of ground in this book! I know your mind is just spinning with hilarious new ideas to try with your hopeless hubby. But it's important we don't just throw you in the deep end - proper training takes time and incremental steps.

That's why I've included some handy exercises to help you implement your comedy-filled training plan. These are scientifically designed to produce optimal results (and laughs!) at each stage.

For example, our "Daily Chore Chart" outlines simple, clear expectations for basic tasks like laundry, dishes, and toilet cleaning. Make several copies - chances are your husband will 'accidentally' lose the first few.

The "Dinner Preparation IQ Test" assesses important skills like using appliances, reading recipes, and finding ingredients. It's best to start easy - level 1 features microwavable foods and ready-made sides.

And the "Bedroom Satisfaction Survey" quantifies your satisfaction on a scale of 1-10 for various romantic techniques. It provides helpful guidance for clueless husbands, like circling 2/10 on "Foreplay" with a note to "See Chapter 3."

With the worksheets, mnemonic devices, and hilarious homework assignments in this appendix, you'll be well equipped to guide your husband's training. Just remember, have patience and keep laughing - you've got this!"

Appendix 2: Recommended Comedic Reading List

"Here are some of my favorite books, movies, and TV shows to get you in the mood for training your hopeless hubby with hilarity:

- 'The Taming of the Shrew' by Shakespeare - a classic comedy about an unruly husband in need of taming.

- 'Everybody Loves Raymond' - nonstop laughs watching Raymond's wife Debra train her bumbling husband.

- 'The Awakening of Mrs. Henderson' - charming 1950s film where Mrs. Henderson's woman's club trains their husbands in etiquette. Hijinks ensue.

- 'How to Train Your Dragon' - an animated delight with lessons that apply to training your husband too. Plus, dragons are similar to men.

- 'The Surrendered Wife' by Laura Doyle - don't let the serious title fool you, this book provides plenty of fodder for laughs.

Immerse yourself in these and you'll be brimming with inspiration for your own brand of husband training humor. Just imagine the look on his face when you nonchalantly ask him to fetch your 'dragon saddle' or lend you his copy of 'The Taming of the Shrew!'"

Appendix 3: Glossary of Husband-Training Terms

"Every expedition needs a map, and every journey needs a guide. Here are some key terms to elucidate your husband training:

Alpha wife - The pack leader. Wields authority over the household with strength and wisdom. Not to be confused with nagging.

Begging - An advanced technique where the wife requests nicely and the husband complies. Requires extensive training.

Dragon saddle - A wife's favorite chair or preferred spot on the couch. Not to be occupied by the husband without express permission.

Fetching - The proper term for a husband retrieving objects for his wife, such as snacks, the remote, or a fresh margarita.

Heel - A command for the husband to come to his wife's side promptly. Preferred over shouting across the house.

Kennel - Where the husband sleeps if he has been particularly naughty. Just kidding! (Or am I?)

Roll over - A trick where the husband shows his belly in submission, acknowledging his wife's supreme authority. Not to be confused with literal rolling on the floor.

Stay - The husband remains in place until given further direction. Useful during football games and chick flicks.

Treats - Motivational rewards for good behavior, like watching a preferred TV show, going golfing, or enjoying a nice steak. Even husbands deserve treats sometimes!

Now you're fluent in husband training lingo. Enjoy peppering these terms into your daily life for added laughs. It's all in good fun of course - but a bit of conditioning never hurts anyone!"

Appendix 4: Bonus Tips for a Happy Marriage

As much as this has been satire, the truth is I want you to have the best marriage possible. Here are some heartfelt tips:

- Express your love and appreciation daily. Don't withhold affection as punishment.

- Allow your partner space to be themselves. Don't try to change their core being.

- Compromise when needed. Marriage requires teamwork.

- Share the workload at home. Don't nitpick if it's not done your way.

- Give each other the benefit of the doubt. Assume positive intent.

- Make intimacy a priority. Don't let the spark fade.

- Keep laughing together! Humor and playfulness strengthen bonds.

Of course, you'll face challenges, but try to tackle them with grace. And never forget why you married this person in the first place. Here's to many more years of happiness!"

Conclusion

After months of training, it's time to reflect on the progress made in transforming your husband into the perfect partner. Though he may not be flawless, you've likely seen improvements in communication, household contributions, date nights, and emotional availability. Pat yourself on the back for a job well done!

Yet the work is never truly finished. A good relationship, like a garden, requires ongoing tending. Don't let the weeds of neglect take root. Continue nurturing intimacy through regular check-ins, new shared experiences, and daily expressions of affection. Complement each other often and give thanks for all you appreciate.

Your comic adventures in husband training were just the beginning. The real reward is a lifetime of love, laughter and companionship. Cherish each moment, even the messy ones. Growth happens through openness, forgiveness and commitment to weathering storms as a team.

This journey brought you closer, revealing new depths of understanding. Now you know your partner's hopes and dreams on a deeper level. Use this insight to support their personal growth. A spouse who feels seen and encouraged will become their best self.

So, take pride in how far you've come, then look ahead to all that's still unfolding. Life with your husband is a continuous journey. Keep your heart open, bring your sense of humor, and enjoy the ride. Your shared destiny is bright with promise. And for the habits that seem impossible to train out of him… you might want to just invest in a couple extra cans of aerosol!

Even with proper training, boys will be boys.

❇ The Ultimate Daily Chore Chart for [Husband's Name]

Dear [Husband's Nickname],

Congratulations! You've been selected as the Official Chore Champion of the Household. Your mission, should you choose to accept it, is to conquer the following tasks and earn brownie points:

🧺 Laundry Duty:

- Goal: Turn your clothes from 'floor art' to 'drawer treasure.'

- Instructions:

   1. Gather dirty laundry (the stuff you've been "saving" for a special occasion).

   2. Load the washing machine (Yes, it's the big, scary box in the laundry room).

   3. Press all the buttons (They're not launching a rocket, promise).

   4. Remember to transfer clothes to the dryer (Don't let them camp out there).

   5. Fold and put away clothes (This is the part where magic happens).

🍴 Dishwashing Delight:

- Goal: Transform the leaning tower of dishes into a sparkling clean oasis.

- Instructions:

1. Tackle the sink full of dishes (No, you can't just hide them in the oven).

2. Channel your inner culinary artist and scrub, rinse, and repeat.

3. Place them back in their natural habitat, the cupboard.

🚽 Toilet Tamer:

- Goal: Conquer the porcelain throne and keep the bathroom fresh.

- Instructions:

1. Equip yourself with cleaning supplies (No, the force isn't enough).

2. Scrub-a-dub-dub, it's toilet time! (Don't forget the seat, rim, and bowl).

3. Flush for victory and leave the bathroom smelling like a bouquet of roses (or at least not like a swamp).

⏰ Time Management Tip:

- Remember, you have 24 hours in a day, and chores only take a fraction of that time!

Rewards:

- Completion of all chores earns you unlimited bragging rights and a high-five.

- Bonus points for creativity (singing while cleaning, wearing a superhero cape, etc.).

Failure to comply:

- Risk of losing access to the TV remote or snacks (The horror!).

Good luck, [Husband's Nickname]! Remember, a happy home is a chore-tastic home. May the chore force be with you!

With love and a sprinkle of dust,

[Your Name]

Dinner Preparation IQ Test

Level 1: The Microwave Master

Dear [Husband's Name],

Welcome to the Dinner Preparation IQ Test - a culinary adventure that will elevate your kitchen skills from zero to hero! Let's start with the basics:

Question 1:

Microwave Mastery

You're tasked with preparing tonight's dinner. Your options: microwaveable foods and ready-made sides. Show us your expertise!

Popcorn – Place the bag in the microwave with the correct side facing up:

a) Label side up

b) Label side down

Frozen Pizza – What's the optimal number of pizza slices to consume while waiting for it to cook?

a) 0 (I have self-control)

b) All of them (obviously)

Instant Mashed Potatoes – Which ingredient should you NOT add for the creamiest texture?

a) Milk

b) Motor oil

Canned Soup – How long should you microwave it for?

a) Until it starts singing "I'm hot stuff!"

b) As per the instructions on the can

Scoring:

4/4: You're a Microwave Maestro!

2-3/4: You're on your way to becoming a kitchen superstar!

0-1/4: Time to rethink your microwave game, buddy!

Level 2: Recipe Detective

Stay tuned for Level 2, where we'll explore the art of following a recipe and locating ingredients. Good luck, aspiring chef!

Bon appétit!

[Your Name]

Feel free to adapt and add more levels as your husband progresses in his culinary journey. The key is to keep it light-hearted and fun!

✵ Bedroom Satisfaction Survey ✵

Dear [Husband's Name],

Welcome to the Bedroom Satisfaction Survey – your key to unlocking the secrets of romantic prowess! Please rate your performance on a scale of 1-10 for the following techniques. Don't worry; it's all good fun!

Technique 1: Setting the Mood

- Lighting, music, ambiance, etc.
- Your Rating (1-10):

Technique 2: Foreplay

- Your magical warm-up routine
- Your Rating (1-10):

📝 Note: If you circled 2/10 or below, please refer to Chapter 3 (or seek further education).

Technique 3: Pillow Talk

   - Sweet nothings and seductive whispers

   - Your Rating (1-10):

Technique 4: Dance Moves

   - Your groove on the dance floor (or bedroom floor)

   - Your Rating (1-10):

Technique 5: Surprise Gestures

   - Thoughtful surprises, gifts, or acts of love

   - Your Rating (1-10):

Technique 6: Communication

   - Openness and understanding

   - Your Rating (1-10):

Technique 7: Bedtime Snacking

   - Snacks and post-romantic activities

   - Your Rating (1-10):

Technique 8: The Big Finish

   - Climaxing on a high note

   - Your Rating (1-10):

Additional Comments or Suggestions

Feel free to share any secret weapons or ideas for bedroom success:

_____

**Overall Satisfaction Rating: **

- 1-5: Needs improvement (We're here to help!)

- 6-8: A solid effort (Keep up the good work!)

- 9-10: Bravo! (You're a bedroom superstar!)

Thank you for participating in the Bedroom Satisfaction Survey. Your efforts are greatly appreciated, and remember, practice makes perfect!

With love and laughter,

[Your Name]

A Note from Your Author:

The names and incidents in this tongue in cheek manual have been completely fictionalized. None of this is guaranteed to work and quite frankly most of it probably won't work.

For those of you who are sick of trying – stay tuned for my next self help training manual titled "How to bury a body where not even the best cadaver dogs can find it."

Happy reading!

About The Author

Tammy L. Brown is a whimsical wordsmith hailing from the charming town of Toccoa, Georgia, nestled snugly in the foothills of the Blue Ridge mountains. While she may have penned this uproarious guide on "How to Train Your Husband," Tammy would like to clarify that she is, in fact, happily married (most days) to a husband who fails to see the humor in this book—a source of endless amusement for her.

In addition to her mischievous marital musings, Tammy also has numerous published books in the delightful world of children's picture books, where her words and illustrations create enchanting tales for young readers. But don't be fooled; she navigates various genres of fiction and nonfiction with equal aplomb, ensuring that her readers are always in for a surprise. When she's not conjuring fictional worlds or attempting to train her husband, Tammy can often be found sipping a Diet Coke (with extra ice) and soaking in the beauty of the Georgia countryside.

So, dear reader, take a moment to revel in Tammy's hilarious advice on husband-honing, but remember, it's all good fun. After all, what's life without a little laughter and a dash of marital mischief?

Printed in Great Britain
by Amazon

32814823R00069